Founders' Agreement
One Hour Startup Toolkit

Tools to Create a Winning Founders Team

Gaurav Narang

Title
Founders' Agreement - One Hour Startup Toolkit

Author
Gaurav Narang

Copyright
©2022 Gaurav Narang
All rights reserved, including the right
to reproduction in whole or in part in any form.

ISBN
979-88-4933-750-0

Publisher
Gaurav Narang

Printed at
Matha Press, Bengaluru

Dedication

Dedicated to my Family

Contents

Dedication 3

Table of Contents 5

Preface 7

Ideal Co-founder 9

Complete Team 12

Is Your Team Complete? 16

Founders Agreement 19

Ownership Structure 20

Guiding Principle 1 – Equity or Salary? 23

Guiding Principle 2 – Financial Needs. 41

Late-stage Co-founder 60

Conflict resolution 81

When a Founder Quits 92

Founders' Agreement Template 114

Annexure A 116

Preface

Are you looking for a co-founder to join your startup but not sure how much equity to share? Are you worried about what will happen if you hire the wrong person on your founding team? How much salary should you take from your startup? How much should your co-founders draw?

Starting a business is tough. It needs multiple skill sets to come together to make a startup successful. Nomatter what your startup idea is, you will need to hire co-founders, probably individuals you have not known or worked with before. Forming the right founding team will be one of the most critical activities that you will undertake, which will make or break your startup.

One Hour Startup Toolkit: The Founders' Agreement covers the aspects related to creating a winning founding team. The book explains key concepts in easy-to-followlanguage with examples, infographics, and tool tips. Thebook's length is kept small on purpose. It should not take more than an hour to read, understand the essentialconcepts, and apply them in your use case.

If you are contemplating forming a startup, if you have created your startup and are looking to hire co- founders, if you are already running a startup but have noclue about what you would do if one of your co-foundersquits,

this book is for you.

Founders' Agreement

Ideal Co-founder

Who will be an ideal co-founder to start your company with? Pause for a moment. Picture two or three individuals with whom you could imagine starting a business together. Chances are, these people are close friends, former colleagues, or perhaps family members. Most likely, the names you have come up with are of those college buddies you've pulled all-nighters with or colleagues you've tackled projects alongside, sharing dreams, goals, and a mutual understanding. These are people who share common ambitions and goals, who understand you, who are compatible with you, who are trustworthy, and whom you would never need to second guess. On the surface, this may indeed be an excellent choice from an interpersonal aspect – a perfect recipe for a harmonious partnership. However, the reality of building a successful startup team demands more than just good vibes. From a functional standpoint, in the long run, starting with this perfectly harmonious team may turn out to be a bad decision.

Let me break it down for you. For a well-balanced founding team, chemistry is indeed essential, but so is physics. Yes, chemistry is crucial — it's the force that binds your team, ensuring everyone is aligned and moving in the same direction, sharing trust, and offering unwavering support. But, let's not underestimate the role of physics here. Like the forces that keep our universe in balance, introducing just the right amount of tension, attraction and dynamism, the founding members of a start-up team should be able to effectively challenge each other, question authority, share criticism, and introduce a healthy dose of friction when the course of action doesn't seem right.

This dynamic will ensure that the team is not just a group of yes-men but a collection of critical thinkers who are comfortable in the art of constructive criticism, ready to spark, manage, and navigate through conflict as it arises. It's through this rigorous process of questioning and challenging each other's ideas that a truly innovative and resilient founding team is forged.

Finding the right balance between chemistry and physics in your team is just the start. What's really crucial is putting together a team that's got it all - a team that can handle all sorts of challenges a startup faces in the early days. This only works if

Founders' Agreement

you're careful about picking a diverse bunch who bring everything you need to the table. So, what do I mean by a "complete team"? Let's dive into that idea now.

Founders' Agreement

Founders' Agreement

Complete Team

Many brilliant entrepreneurs fail because they fail to form the complete team that they would need for their Startup to succeed commercially. Let me share the story of a real-life startup I encountered recently. Three bright and young engineers were behind this Startup. Two loved to code, and the third one was a designer, a perfect combination for creating an appealing software product. All three of them had attended college together and worked on a startup together in the past as well. Their idea was to revolutionize the school education system by building a software product around integrating experiential learning and extra-curricular activities into the school curriculum. After taking around a year and a half to create a beautiful and functional product, they reached out to a handful of schools to offer their solution. Unfortunately, none of the schools seemed interested. So, they finally decided to fold. This was in the year 2019.

Why did they fail? Multiple reasons, primarily three, that I would cover here.

1. They built the entire product without ever checking with their (potential) customers if

they needed it.

2. They did not spend time on understanding the right sales channel for their product. Schools in India are primarily run by not-for-profit trusts or charities. The procurement channels in this kind of setup work in a peculiar fashion, covering which is beyond the scope of this book.

3. They quit too early. The exact number of the handful of schools they visited before deciding to quit was three.

Was it possible to avoid this failure?

Consider an alternative scenario. In this scenario, let us add a fourth co-founder to their team. She comes from a sales background. To be specific, she comes from an educational sales background. She has been selling various products and solutions to schools for the last five years. She is an extrovert. She loves talking, and being amongst people, unlike the three co-founders in our case, who were introverts, loved their laptops and coding, and considered three failed sales call as the view of the broader market. Further, let us assume that she joined them on an equity plus commission-based model without any fixed payout component. She also assisted them in refining their product by setting up meetings with different schools in her network. How, do you think, will the chance of

success for the startup change in this alternative scenario?

Now, let us add a real-world twist into this hypothetical scenario. The event we are talking about is CoVid-19. This crisis forced all schools to go offline and scout for any online model they could get their hands on to stay relevant. So, how likely is it that the Startup would have succeeded in this new reality? Without the hypothetical fourth co-founder, their chances of success probably would not have changed. But with her? That could have been a different story altogether.

Their team was missing some key pieces. For the team to be complete, they needed someone who could fill in the gaps that the three of them could not. They needed someone who understood what the schools were after; someone who knew how to sell to educational institutes, and someone who could talk the talk and walk the walk in marketing their product. If they had brought that fourth co-founder into the mix, the team would have been complete.

Founders' Agreement

Forming a winning team takes batsmen, bowlers, and a wicket keeper.

A team with 11 best batsmen in the world will not get you the cup.

Founders' Agreement

Is Your Team Complete?

Let's circle back to the beginning, to those top picks for co-founders in your mind. Think it through once more. Do they complete your team? Or are they just strengthening it in one area, which is already strong dueto the qualities that you bring to the table? What skills are missing to make your team truly complete?

Does your startup idea revolve around a website? If yes, then you will need a good tech resource who can code like a pro. Or maybe you're diving into fintech? Thena finance wizard is the one who you need by your side. Planning to shake things up in agriculture? You better have someone who knows the ins and outs of farming and crops.

The kind of team you build should mirror the field you're jumping into, like education in our example. But that's just part of the story. The skills you need are also about balancing out who you are. If you are an introvert, find a co-founder who is an extrovert. If you are aneternal optimist (most entrepreneurs are), find someonewho can grab you by the collar and pull you back when you are running headway into an incoming train.

Founders' Agreement

Forming a complete team is not only about technical skill sets.
Personality traits matter as well.

Founders' Agreement

Alright, let's circle back to those few names you've been tossing around in your head. When you put yourselves together, do you visualize a complete, balanced, and winning team; the kind of team you'd bet all your money on? If the answer is No, and in 98 out of 100 cases, it will be a resounding 'NO', you do need to find the right co-founders to complete your team. It's now time to think beyond the two or three names you had initially come up with.

But there is a problem again. Most of the individuals that you can imagine working together with are your friends whom you can trust and who are like you. They don't bring anything different to the table; they mirror your skills and ways of thinking, which is probably why you all get along so well in the first place. Sure, you know folks with the skills you're missing, but they're more like acquaintances, or maybe you've just heard of them through someone else. How can you induct such an individual into your founding team? There are a zillion things that can go wrong. Isn't it?

Yes, you're spot on, and that's exactly where a founders' agreement comes into play. It's your safety net for when you're ready to take that leap with someone who's not in your immediate circle

Founders' Agreement

but has the exact skills your team needs to win.

Founders Agreement

Founders' agreement, as the name suggests, is a formal agreement among the founding members of a startup's team. Although not yet widely adopted within the Indian startup ecosystem, in more mature markets, such an agreement is often deemed essential, with investors typically requiring its presence before agreeing to fund your startup.

A founders agreement covers, amongst other things, the roles and responsibilities, the ownership structure, the investment contribution, the conflict resolution mechanism, and multiple other scenarios that may arise in future. For your reference, a sample template of the founders' agreement is included in Annexure A. You can go through it when you need it. But, for now, let's spend some time exploring a few crucial aspects that should be covered in a founder's agreement.

Founders' Agreement

Ownership Structure

The proverbial question. Who gets how much? How do you split the pie? Is there extra credit for coming up with the idea, or what about the co-founder who's not all-in full-time — should her slice be smaller? And then there's the question of money. If one co-founder is investing more cash, does that mean she should get a bigger cut? What about the prestige of education — does an Ivy League tag weigh more than others? And let's not forget skills. Should a finance guru get more than an engineer? Or consider the scenario where one co-founder is leaving a well-paid gig to dive into this venture, while the others are just stepping out of college or haven't worked at all. How to create a fair split, then?

All of these are valid questions and well-intentioned too. And yes, they can be awkward to bring up, especially if you're planning to start up with long-time buddies. But dodge them, and you're setting yourself up for trouble. Everyone in the team needs to be clear on what they're getting and what the expectations are — it keeps the focus on the shared vision rather than on individual gains or losses. The tough truth? There's no one-size-fits-all answer to these dilemmas. In the following sections, I'll toss in my two cents on some of these topics, drawing from my own journey and what I've seen in the startup arena. Think of these insights as a starting point, something to spark discussion. You can take them, leave them, or tweak them to fit your situation.

Irrespective of what you choose to do with other inputs, there are two guiding principles that I would recommend sticking to while answering these questions.

- Guiding principle 1 – Treat equity and salary separately.
- Guiding Principle 2 – Don't question financial needs.

Founders' Agreement

Founders' Agreement

Guiding Principle 1 – Equity or Salary?

Every entrepreneur with faith in their vision knows the real gold lies in the ownership stake of the company, not the paycheck they cash in the early days. If your potential co-founders are hung up on salary rather than equity, it's a red flag—they might not be cut out for the co-founder journey. Instead, they could be a great fit as early-stage employees, a topic we'll dive into later. For now, in the guiding principle one, we will only talk about equity ownership.

When deciding how to split equity among co-founders, a few of the important parameters that you may want to factor in are:

1. Capital contribution – How much cash is each person putting in?

2. Time contribution – Is everyone on board full-time, or are some only able to commit part-time?

3. Opportunity cost – What are they giving up to join the venture? This could be a steady salary, or another job offer.

4. Experience level – How does each person's experience weigh into the equity equation?

Founders' Agreement

5. Skill set – How vital are their skills to the startup's success, and are these skills hard to find?

6. Idea premium – Should there be a premium for the idea?

7. Pedigree premium – should there be a premium for the big brands – schools, or companies that one has been to?

Before sharing my opinion on these matters, I would submit that in situations like these, one should not be guided by greed but by a sense of fairness and equity. Forget all the negotiation books or lectures you may have attended that teach you to get the maximum out of any negotiation. If you somehow manage to do that, it may ensure short-term success. Still, it will eventually lead to a failure in the long run, not only for the team but also for the business.

Founders' Agreement

Founders' Agreement

Rule of Thumb

Treat your fellow founders as you would want them to treat you.

Think of entering a co-founder agreement like entering a marriage. It's all about fairness and balance. An intent to gain more will eventually lead to the relationship's failure. When in doubt, you should go the extra mile to be fair to your partner than risk losing a relationship for something that will eventually amount to nibbles in the larger scheme of things. Having understood the philosophy, I am coming from; you will be able to understand the logic behind my views on how these questions should be tackled. Of course, take my advice only if it resonates with you.

Let's tackle these factors one by one.

Capital Contribution

This is the simplest one. The equity split should be in direct proportion to the investment contribution. So, for example, if one partner brings in 30% of the funds and another 70%, the split should be 30:70.

Time contribution

This is a tricky one. Running a startup is a full-time job. When I say full-time, I do mean that you're on the clock 24/7. It isn't your typical 9-to-5 gig, 5 days a week. Seriously, it's an all-in or nothing deal. If someone's not ready to dive in full-time, one does

Founders' Agreement

not deserve to be on the founders' team.

That is my curt opinion, but when I share this with aspiring entrepreneurs, I get a range of reasons for why they cannot move forward without a part-time co- founder. Sometimes, these reasons are a bit flimsy, but other times they're totally legit, often boiling down to the part-timer's financial needs. So, what do you do in this situation? Here are a couple of strategies that might work:

Approach 1

Make provision for paying a modest salary to that co-founder and get them to jump in full-time. We will dig deeper into this when we discuss the second guiding principle in a while.

Approach 2

If they're only able to come on board part-time, think of them more like investors rather than co-founders. Here's what I mean: if a part-time founder is also kicking in some cash and looking after certain tasks while holding down another job, don't view their cash as founder's equity right off the bat. Consider it more like an investor's stake and then offer them an additional share for the tasks they will be handling part-time. Let's say you and your co-founder are contributing `100,000 each. If both of you were working full-time, the equity split would be 50:50, right? Now, consider the scenario in which one of you will be working part-time with a promise to join full-time soon. In this case, evaluate what equity the two of you would be willing to share with an investor who would give `100,000 to you today. For simplicity's sake, let us say that number is 10%. In this case, initially treat your partner as that early-stage equity investor. The equity split will now be 90:10 in favour of the co-founder working full-time.

However, if you stop here, it will be unfair to your partner as she will be working part-time for the Startup and will also be handling a few responsibilities independently. She is also looking forward to joining you soon. It will be fair on your part to hand her an additional premium for her non-monetary contribution in the early stage. Let us say you will share another 5% for the responsibilities that your partner will be handling part- time. This improvisation changes the split from 90:10 to 85:15, which is fairer as compared to a 50:50 or a 90:10 split. However, this leads to another issue. A 15% share is too low for your partner to feel motivated. In the long run, you want her to remain motivated and look forward to coming on board in a full-time role. In fact, if you could have your way or had enough financial backing, you want her to join

Founders' Agreement

full-time right now. So, throw in an extra incentive, a large one, provided she transitions to full- time role within a set time frame. Say, 25% if she joins full-time in one year, 15% if in two, and nothing after that. With this clause included, post one year, if she does join full time, the split will be 60:40; if she joins after two years, it will be 70:30. If she is not with you even after a couple of years, she was never meant to be, and the 5% share that she got in an early-stage startup for her part-time work is more than fair (she got another 10% against money and was treated at par with any other investor at that stage).

Opportunity Cost

Here's the thing about startups: when you're looking at what you're giving up in terms of salary versus what you could gain in equity, there's no real contest.

Think about it. In a startup that hits it big, the money you make from owning a piece of the company dwarfs whatever you could have earned in salary. We're talking a massive difference. For most entrepreneurs, the salary is just a tiny fraction of what they end up making from their equity stake. So, if you're wrestling with how to balance giving up a sure thing (like a salary) for a piece of the action (equity), know that betting on equity is where the real reward lies. As such, offering a higher premium in equity for salary foregone does not make much sense. We will cover more on this subject when we discuss thesecond guiding principle shortly.

Experience Level

When we're talking about how much experience each person brings to the table, it's pretty straightforward. If everyone's more or less on the same level, experience- wise, then it's not something you need to lose sleep over. However, in case of a significant difference in experience levels of, say, more than 4-5 years, a small premiumof, say, less than 5% may be attributed to a co-founder with a higher experience level. It's a way to recognize the value of the insights and knowledge that come with those additional years of experience.

Skill Set

When it comes down to valuing specific skills in a startup, it's a bit of a grey area. How much more should one skill set weigh over another? It's a valid question, but it's not one with straightforward answers. Let's walkthrough a couple of scenarios to get a better grip on this.

Scenario 1

Picture a startup that's all about robotics. There are two co-founders: one is a robotics wizard with a professional degree and a whole decade of experience under her belt. The other co-founder is more of a businessperson who will bring in the business and raise funds. She has been in robotics sales for a little over three years. In this case, how should the equity be divided? They could go halves, recognizing each other's contributions equally, or they might decide to tip the scales a bit—say, up to 10% more for the one with the deeper technical expertise.

Scenario 2

In the second scenario, the example remains the same, but in this case, both co-founders have decade-long experience in their respective domains. One might argue that since robotics is at the heart of the startup, the co- founder with the technical know-how should command a higher premium. While that sounds reasonable at first glance, it doesn't necessarily pan out in the long run. Once the robotics product is developed, the business will need the skill set of selling and fundraising; as such, this skill set will be equally, if not more important. Remember the school software product example we discussed? That business failed because of the lack of a non-technical skill

Founders' Agreement

set. In scenario 2, an equal equity split makes the most sense.

Take a good look at those two scenarios we just talked about. You will notice that the difference in equity in the first scenario really comes down to how much more experience one co-founder has over the other. But when we level the playing field in terms of experience in the second scenario, that extra slice of the pie for experience disappears. So, what am I getting at? Is it fair to say that no particular skill set, or expertise should get a premium over another? My take is: Yes.

If a skill set is critical enough to have someone on the founders' team, then every skill deserves equal respect. If the skill set is not important enough for the Startup, or if the skill is readily available for hire, and you can afford it, hire it rather than getting the individual on the founding team.

Businesses evolve; what's essential today might not be the priority tomorrow, and something else could become the next big thing. Take our robotics startup: once the gizmo's built, being able to sell it and keep the lights on becomes the new priority. Or imagine running low on cash mid-development. Without someone who knows how to bring in funds, that cool robot might never see the light of day. So, discounting someone's expertise

Founders' Agreement

because it seems less relevant at a particular moment is a big mistake. Trying to do that may create artificial barriers and fissures in a team which will do more harm than good in the long run.

Even if one of the co-founders feels short-changed by a small percentage point here or there, one should think of it as an investment in team harmony and the startup's future success. It's a small price to pay for long-term bonhomie and success of the venture.

Idea premium

I firmly believe there should be no premium for an idea. Many first-time entrepreneurs, before they start building a startup, allot a very high premium to the idea. They guard it like a treasure, unwilling to share or seek out feedback. The fear? Someone else might copy it. Now, if you've got something truly groundbreaking that could be patented, that's a different story. But if your big idea is just a new twist on solving an old problem, or if you are just copy-pasting a successful model from somewhere else to your market, then allotting any premium to the idea itself doesn't make much sense.

Here's the real deal: it is not just about what your idea is; it is about how will you bring it to life,

Founders' Agreement

Founders' Agreement

that will determine whether you will succeed or fail. Execution is king. Clinging to your idea without testing it out in the real world, without gathering real customer insights, you would likely end up spending way more time and resources, in developing something, than necessary. And worse, you might end up with a product or service that nobody actually wants.

Rather than keeping your idea under wraps, why not tap into the collective brainpower around you? Talk about it, get feedback, see what others think. This approach will not only sharpen your idea but also save you from heading down a dead-end path. Remember, in the end, it is how well you execute your idea that will make or break your startup.

Every idea is a work in progress, and trust me, it's going to evolve. A lot of the tweaking and fine-tuning comes from the nitty-gritty of actually getting your hands dirty putting the idea into action and listening to the feedback from the first early adopters. Expect to go through quite a few versions before you hit on something that really works. This will usually be the case for innovative models that are not simple copy-paste of successful models from similar markets abroad.

In many cases, the final idea that clicks may not

evenbe remotely related to the initial idea. All these changes will take multiple iterations and considerable amount of time. Over time, as you and your co-founders dive into the development process, tweak things here, adjust things there, based on real-world experience and feedback, the idea will start to take a real shape.

Every co-founder's input, every bit of feedback, every failure, and every success along the way contributesto molding that initial spark into a viable business. So, when it comes down to it, does it make sense to put extra value on being the person who first said, "Hey, I've got an idea"? Not at all. What matters is how you all work together to turn that idea into something tangible and successful.

Pedigree premium

When it comes to picking who is in your startup's founding team, there is no room for a "pedigree premium." You are not bringing people on board because of the fancy schools they attended or the big-name companies they have worked for. What really matters? Their skills, what they can do, how they think, and their drive to make things happen.

Sure, a prestigious background can turn heads,

Founders' Agreement

but at the end of the day, it is about what each person brings to the table—their ability to tackle problems, innovate, and push the startup forward. So, forget about logos and diplomas; focus on the real deal: talent, grit, and the right attitude. That is what builds a strong foundation for your startup.

Guiding Principle 2 – Financial Needs.

When people come together to start a new venture, they are all coming from different walks of life. Their financial situations are not the same—some might have a cushion of savings, while others are living paycheck to paycheck. One co-founder might have a family relying on them, another might be single with fewer financial burdens, and another might be supporting not just themselves but their parents or even extended family. Everyone's circumstances will be different, and it may not practically be possible for the co-founders to step into each other's shoes and understand the specific situation of everyone.

Given this mix of personal financial situations, trying to tailor individual compensation plans for each co- founder can get complicated. A more straightforward strategy is to settle on a universal rule that everyone follows, especially in the early days. Initially, expect that everyone will be taking home less than what they might earn elsewhere. The idea is that once the startup begins to find its footing, either by generating enough revenue or securing investment, then compensation can be adjusted to more closely match the market standard. But, until that happens, the reality is that salaries are going to be on the lower side.

There are a couple of ways to approach this

Founders' Agreement

Approach 1

In the first approach everyone agrees to take a similar cut based on what they used to make. Let us say the cut is 70% on existing salary (or opportunity cost) in year one, 60% in year two (or on achieving a specific business goal or revenue target), 50% in year three and likewise till the business can afford market salaries, either out of profits or investments. For example, if there are three co-founders who were earning ₹120,000, ₹90,000, and ₹30,000, respectively, per month. In this approach, they will take home ₹36,000, ₹27,000 and ₹9,000 per month in year one. ₹48,000, ₹36,000 and ₹12,000 per month in year two and so on.

Do you see the problem with this approach? There are two. The first and most evident problem is that the co-founder taking home ₹9,000 a month will find it extremely hard to make ends meet. She may continue to be on board and use her savings for a few months, or a year, or two at max. But, unless the startups' fortunes change fast, the financial stress will force her to drop out.

Founders' Agreement

Another not-so-evident problem with this approach is that this is retrospective in nature. It bases everyone's pay on their past jobs, not on what they are bringing to the startup here and now. It doesn't matter if one co-founder is putting in more effort or bringing more value to the table; their compensation is tied to what they used to do, not what they are going to do in the future. That is hardly motivating, and it does not encourage anyone to really push the envelope or go the extra mile compared to their teammates.

Approach 2

The second approach would be to offer the same salary to everyone. Consider the same example. Let us say that the number agreed for everyone is ₹30,000 in year one and ₹40,000 in year two. In this scenario, each co-founder will draw ₹30,000 in year one, irrespective of their individual opportunity cost. This will ensure that there is no distinction between team members, and it sends a clear message that every co-founder's efforts are seen as equally valuable. This will also ensure that each co-founder will be able to meet their basic financial needs.

But, just like our first approach, this one is not without its drawbacks. Again, we are treating everyone's future contributions as equal, no matter how much they actually put into the startup. And here is another hiccup: for the co-founder who is used to a much higher salary, this equal pay model could be a tough pill to swallow. Imagine going from the highest salary to the same as everyone else. That is a 75% pay cut for our top earner, while for the person who was already around the ₹30,000 mark, there is no cut at all.

So, which of the two approaches is superior? Maybe none is. Both ways have their pros and cons, but there is one good thing with both the approaches: they do not alter how much of the company each co-founder owns. That means when it comes to the big picture—those long-term gains and the chance to build something truly valuable—the team's interests stay aligned.

If everyone's coming from similar financial situations, our second approach, the flat salary one, could work out just fine. But if you have got a diverse group with different financial needs and backgrounds, you might need a mix-and-match approach. In such a scenario, a hybrid solution could offer the flexibility to address everyone's needs without stirring up resentment or devaluing anyone's contribution.

Hybrid Approach

Let us now mix the two approaches and come up with a hybrid approach. In this method, we will try to strike a balance by applying a similar percentage cut across the board, but with a twist: there is a floor to how low anyone's salary can go. This means everyone gets at least a certain minimum amount, no matter what.

For example, in the hybrid approach in the above example, if we consider the percentage pay cuts of 70% and 60% from the Approach 1 and the fixed payout of a salary of a minimum of ₹30,000 from the Approach 2, then the payouts for the three co-founders will be ₹36,000, ₹30,000 and ₹30,000 in year one. Then, in the second year, they'd see an increase to ₹48,000, ₹36,000, and ₹30,000. This hybrid model might just hit the sweet spot between the two standalone approaches, offering a fairer distribution that considers both the need for equal treatment and the reality of differing financial situations.

Irrespective of how one decides the salary structure initially, one should understand that any of these arrangements are temporary and would last only till a serious investor comes on board or till the company can afford to pay market salaries.

Founders' Agreement

In either scenario, the startup board will eventually link the payment structure to the market scenario and the expected future value of each co-founder going forward.

Let us now take an example to apply the concepts wehave learned so far.

Example

Let us take a hypothetical scenario wherein Jack, Mary, and Som come together to start a game-changing venture. Their big idea? To launch an affordable, on- demand ambulance service. They are thinking of kicking things off in Agra and then expanding from there post a successful pilot of the model. Here's a snapshot of whothey are and what they bring to the table:

- Jack is the medic of the group, with six years of experience bouncing between four hospitals in Agra. He is earning ₹50,000 a month and plans to weave a network of hospitals into their service while keeping his day job.

- Mary is all about coding and will be the brain behind the app that lets people summon an ambulance with a tap. She is ditching her app development job, which she held for the last 3 years and wherein she pulls in ₹100,000 a month, to dive into this full-time. Along with developing the app, she will also be the one responsible for handling customers.

- Som is a fleet operator with a taxi rental company. He will create a network of ambulance operators who will be tied up with the Startup. He will also be responsible for ensuring safe pick-up, transit, and the patient's arrival at the nearest hospital. He has been working for the last two years, and his current salary is ₹40,000 per month. He will be leaving his job and working full-time along with Mary.

The initial capital they have put together is ₹20,00,000, of which jack is bringing in ₹5,00,000, Mary is contributing ₹4,00,000, Som is contributing ₹1,00,000, and another ₹10,00,000 is coming from an investor who is taking a 10% share for her investment.

Given what we have understood so far about equity, salary, and the whole startup dynamics, how should the three divide up the ownership? Let's break it down, step by step, keeping in mind everything from their contributions, roles, to the sacrifices they are making to get this off the ground.

Founders' Agreement

For the first 3 years of its operations 2008 to 2011, Uber restrcited its services to the city of San Franciso. In the next three, it scaled internationally.

Uber

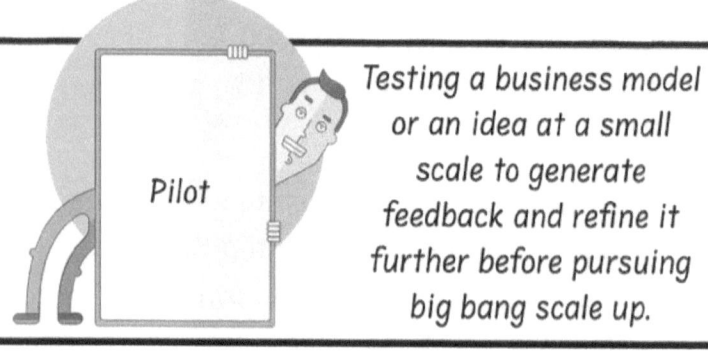

Pilot — Testing a business model or an idea at a small scale to generate feedback and refine it further before pursuing big bang scale up.

Founders' Agreement

Equity Split

Step 1 – Capital Contribution

Based on the capital contribution model, the amount of equity split should be directly linked to the amount of money each individual brings in. The investor is taking a 10% stake for her ₹10,00,000. This means that 90% of the company's equity is left to be split between Jack, Mary, and Som according to the cash they have each contributed - ₹5,00,000 by Jack, ₹4,00,000 by Mary, and ₹1,00,000 by Som.

Based on this information, here's how the company's ownership initially breaks down.

	Jack	Mary	Som	Investor
Contribution	5,00,000	4,00,000	1,00,000	10,00,000
Equity (%age)	45%	36%	9%	10%

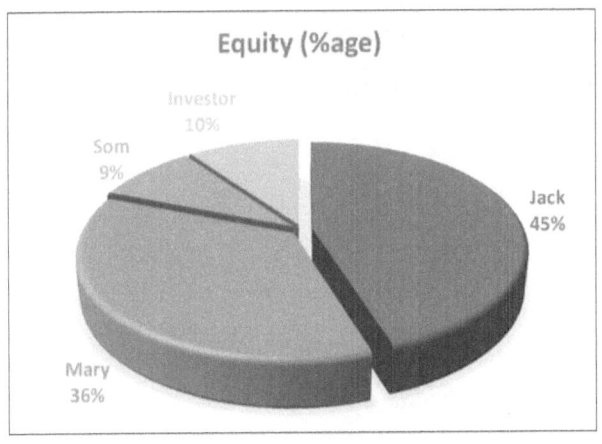

Step 2 – Time Contribution

Based on the given case facts, we know that Jack will not be working full time; as such, his monetary contribution cannot be treated at par with the capital that other co-founders are bringing in. Instead, his contribution should be treated at par with the other early-stage investor. By that logic, Jack should get 5% inlieu of the ₹5,00,000 that he is contributing.

But wait, Jack is not just tossing in cash; he is also going to play a big role in the initial days of the company. He is the one who will be setting up the whole hospital network. Plus, Jack has got the medical expertise and contacts that are pretty much gold for a startup like this. Recognizing the value that Jack will be bringing beyond his share of cash, Mary and Som decide to allocate another 5% for his time contribution. With this tweak, the ownership structure now gets revised and fairer than it was before. Take a look.

	Jack	Mary	Som	Investor
Contribution	5,00,000	4,00,000	1,00,000	10,00,000
Equity (%age)	10%	64%	16%	10%
Comment	Part Time	Full Time	Full Time	NA

Founders' Agreement

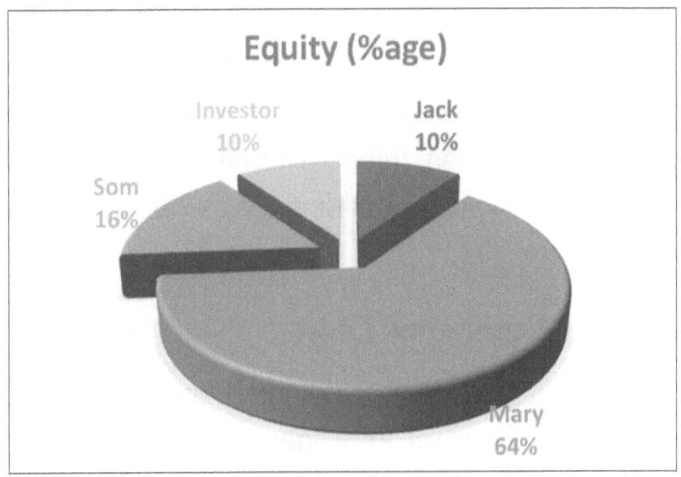

Step 3 – Opportunity Cost

In our setup, Mary and Som are all in, dedicating their full energy to the startup, while Jack is balancing this venture with his regular job. Since Jack is holding on to his day job, his opportunity cost can be evaluated only against the time that he will be putting in which has already been compensated for in the previous step. So, for now, let's focus on Mary and Som.

Both Mary and Som are experts in their fields, each bringing something special and hard-to-find, to the table. Respecting each other's skill set and talent, they should not let their potential earnings outside the startup influence how they divide the

Founders' Agreement

equity. They are in this together. The right thing to do for them will be to value each other's commitment and skills over anything they might be giving up by being a part of the startup. This decision will keep things simple and focused on what they would be building, not what they would be missing.

Step 4 – Experience Level

When it comes to past experience, out of the three, Jack has got an edge. Jack's advantage is not just about his years of experience being almost double; it is more about how his expertise and connections are highly relevant and vital for getting the startup off the ground. Recognizing this, Mary and Som decide to offer a little extra to Jack— say, a 3% extra for bringing that valuable experience to the team. As for Mary and Som, their experience levels are pretty much on par with each other, so they figure there is no need to split hairs over it.

With this the ownership structure gets revised.

	Jack	Mary	Som	Investor
Contribution	5,00,000	4,00,000	1,00,000	10,00,000
Equity (%age)	13.0%	61.6%	15.4%	10.0%
Comment	6 Years	3 Years	2 Years	NA

Founders' Agreement

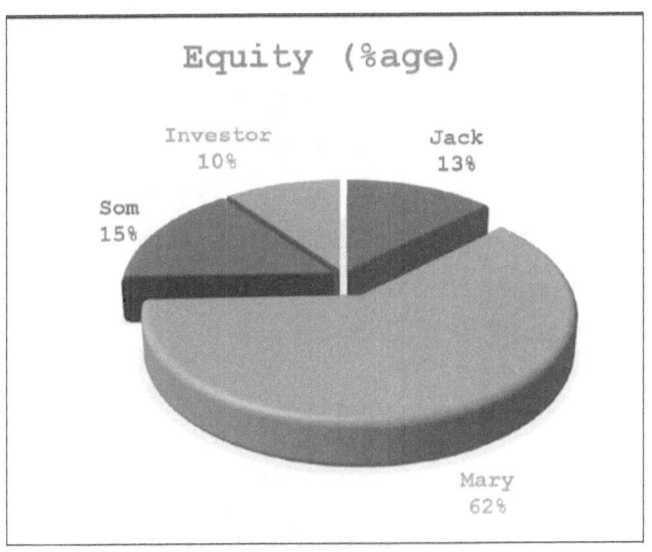

Step 5 – Skill Set

Jack, Mary, and Som each have their own unique set of skills that they bring to the startup. Every single one of these skills is absolutely key to making the business fly. That is why they have decided not to play favorites or give extra points to any one person based on their skills alone. Everyone's contribution is seen as equally vital to the startup's success, so there is no bonus equity just for having a particular skill set.

Step 6 – Idea Premium

Jack, Mary, and Som have all flipped through the pages of this book, taking to heart the advice given. So, when it came time to talk about who came up with the idea, they all agreed: no extra credit or equity just for being the idea person. They understand that it is the teamwork and execution that really bring a startup to life, not just the spark of the initial idea.

Step 7 – Pedigree Premium

Jack, Mary, and Som all agreed that where they went to college wouldn't factor into how they split the equity. It doesn't matter if someone's diploma comes from an Ivy League or a state school; they're all accomplished professionals who are doing fairly well in their chosen fields. So, they decided not to allocate any extra shares for having a fancy college name on resume.

So, after all is said and done, we've got the table that lays out how Jack, Mary, and Som decided to divvy up the equity of their startup.

	Jack	Mary	Som	Investor
Contribution	5,00,000	4,00,000	1,00,000	10,00,000
Equity (%age)	13.0%	61.6%	15.4%	10.0%

Founders' Agreement

Do you think they have reached a fair split? How would you have sliced the pie if you were in their shoes? And here is something to chew on: would your method of splitting equity have been any different before you read these pages? If there is a gap between your before and after, that means this book managed to clear up some of the fog surrounding equity and the whole startup partnership saga in your mind. If you are seeing things ina new light, then I am glad this effort made a difference, even if just a little.

Salary Split

Now that we have got the equity split all sorted, there is another big question on the table: How much salary should Mary and Som draw from the pool of ₹20,00,000 that the Startup has put together? It is time to talk numbers and figure out what makes sense for their paychecks.

Let us consider all three approaches that we had laidout, one by one.

Approach 1

In the first approach, everyone takes a fixed percentage cut on their current salary. Let us say that Mary and Som agree for the cut to be 60%. In that case, this is how their salaries will look like before and after they join the Startup.

	Current Salary	Cut	Startup Salary
Mary	1,00,000	60%	40,000
Som	40,000	60%	16,000
Comment	Fixed cut of 60%		

Approach 2

In the second approach, Mary and Som decide to take home a fixed payout of ₹30,000. It is straightforward, equal, and simplifies the decision-making process. This is what their salaries will look like in this case.

	Current Salary	Cut	Startup Salary
Mary	1,00,000	NA	30,000
Som	40,000	NA	30,000
Comment	Fixed and equal salary for both		

Approach 3

In approach three, which is a hybrid approach, both Mary and Som agree to take a cut of 60%, subject to the fact that neither of them should take home less than a fixed sum of ₹30,000 per month. In this case, this is how their salaries will look like before and after they join the Startup.

	Current Salary	Cut	Startup Salary
Mary	1,00,000	60%	40,000
Som	40,000	60%	30,000
Comment	Fixed cut with minimum salary		

The third approach is probably the best for Mary and Som to follow in this case. One may be left with the feeling that Mary is getting shortchanged here but as the cuts will continue to get lower in progressive years (say 50% in year 2 and 30% in year 3), the variance will reduce.

	Current Salary	Cut Y1	Salary Y1	Cut Y2	Salary Y2	Cut Y3	Salary Y3
Mary	1,00,000	60%	40,000	50%	50,000	30%	70,000
Som	40,000	60%	30,000	50%	30,000	30%	30,000
Comment	Fixed cut with minimum salary						

Founders' Agreement

Okay, we have got a plan that seems a lot fairer now. But hold on a sec, there is a snag in this setup. Do you notice it? Som is stuck with a ₹30,000 salary for three whole years straight. Meanwhile, the world won't stand still—prices for just about everything will likely creep up, thanks to inflation. Doesn't it make sense to factor in a yearly raise to keep up with those rising costs? Absolutely.

Let us pencil in a 10% inflation adjustment on that minimum salary. With this tweak, the salary structure for Som (and Mary, if it applies to her too) will evolve more smoothly over time. This approach not only feels right but also keeps the peace by making sure neither Som nor Mary feels short-changed as expenses climb. Here is how the revised numbers could play out, aiming for a setup that is more in tune with both of their needs and helps sidestep any brewing resentment as the startup grows.

	Current Salary	Cut Y1	Salary Y1	Cut Y2	Salary Y2	Cut Y3	Salary Y3
Mary	1,00,000	60%	40,000	50%	50,000	30%	70,000
Som	40,000	60%	30,000	50%	33,000	30%	36,300
Comment	Fixed cut with minimum salary + 10% annual increment in min salary						

Up to now, we have discussed about how to split

ownership when everyone jumps into the startup boat at the same time. But life is not always that straightforward, right? Sometimes, a new co-founder might tag along after things have already kicked off. Or, on the flip side, one of the original crew might decide to bail. Either way, these shifts can really shake up the whole ownership puzzle among the founding team.

Next up, we are going to tackle these twists and turns. We will look into what happens to the equity and the team dynamic when someone new comes on board or when someone decides it is time to exit the stage. Navigating these changes is crucial for keeping things fair and focused as your startup evolves.

Late-stage Co-founder

So far, we have explored the division of ownership among co-founders at the startup's inception. But what about the scenarios where changes happen in the founding team after the initial setup—specifically, departures and new additions during later stages of the startup's development? Let me explain with an example.

Let's say you were fortunate enough to find a worthy co-founder and shared a fair split with her. Somehow things did not work out between you, and your co-founder decided to quit. What should happen to the equity she already holds in the company in such a situation? If the initial split between you and her was 50:50, she now owns 50% of the company. She is free to walk away, earn a living outside, and enjoy the fruits of your efforts as you continue to scale the company up. Not a fair scenario indeed.

Conversely, how should one handle introduction of a new co-founder into an already established startup? This venture has moved beyond its early stages, having validated its business model, acquired paying customers, and successfully navigated initial challenges.

Determining an equitable share for a new co-founder at this juncture could be tough.

In this section, we aim to address these complex scenarios, providing insights into how equity can be adjusted fairly when co-founders either leave or join thestartup after its formation.

Scenario 1 – Mid-term Quit

Dealing with ownership when a founder leaves partway through the journey is tricky. A founder may quit due to multiple reasons. For example, she may lose faith in the business idea. She may get a better opportunity elsewhere. She may leave due to an interpersonal conflict with another founder. A medical emergency may render her unfit to perform her role. She may quit due to a family emergency. God forbid, a co-founder's untimely demise can also lead to the situation of a co-founder quitting in between. Should we handle all these situations with a blanket approach, or does each warrant a different response?

Irrespective of how you handle a co-founder' departure, her equity stake will be a difficult issue to deal with. How do you reclaim shares from someone who legally owns them? Convincing a departing co-founder to give up her stake isn't straightforward. This is where the idea of equity vesting comes into play, offering a structured way to manage such scenarios.

Equity vesting, put simply, means that while you might officially own a certain percentage of a company from the start, you actually earn this ownership gradually over time. For instance, if a founder is supposed to own 60% but there is a four-year vesting schedule, leaving after two years means only securing half of that stake—30% of the company, or 15% for each year she has contributed. If the exit happens after just one year, then she would only take away 15% of the company, representing 25% of her intended 60% share.

With this vesting framework in mind, let us circle back to our initial dilemma. When a co-founder is set to leave, does the reason behind her departure influence how we handle their vested equity? I would say Yes. In order to understand my reasoning better, it will be helpful to categorize the myriad reasons a founder might leave into four broad categories.

Founders' Agreement

Voluntary Leave

Voluntary leave happens when a co-founder decides to step down on her own, not due to any pressing business crisis, emergency, or life-altering event. Instead, the decision stems from personal reasons—perhaps a new opportunity has caught her eye, or her belief in the business has waned. Essentially, her reasons to leave are internal, not triggered by any external circumstances.

In this case, any shares not yet vested are forfeited. But the real question is about the vested shares. Departing while the startup is on an upward trajectory can potentially slow down its growth, even if it does not derail it entirely.

Exiting a co-founding role isn't typically a snap decision. It is often the culmination of much thought and deliberation, balancing the positives against the negatives over time. If the departing co-founder has been open about her thought process and has actively helped find and train a suitable replacement, her approach can be seen as responsible and mature. In such situations, it is only fair that she retains the equity she has rightfully earned.

However, if this departure catches you off guard, particularly if it is abrupt and without regard for the impact on the startup's future, it is understandable to feel betrayed. The knee-jerk reaction might be to enforce a penalty for such exits, but given that the very concept of vesting anticipates the possibility of early departures, this might be unjust to your cofounder.

A more equitable solution could be to include a stipulation in the founders' agreement for an extended transition—say, a six-month period wherein Equity does not continue to vest. During this time, the co-founder who is leaving would dedicate herself to minimizing any negative effects on the startup, ensuring a smooth handover and continuity of growth. This approach balances fairness with practicality, maintaining the relationship and integrity of the founding team.

Emergency Leave

Imagine if a co-founder has to bow out because of an unforeseen emergency that leaves her unable to fulfill her responsibilities—like a serious health issue, a major accident, or a personal crisis such as a divorce or the loss of someone close. These are situations completely beyond her control, forcing her to step away from her role in the startup.

Under these circumstances, it's only fair that she keeps any shares that have already vested, acknowledging her contributions up to that point. But, as for the shares that haven't yet vested, those would go back to the company. This approach respects the time and effort she has invested while recognizing her current inability to continue contributing.

Forced Leave due to policy violation

Imagine if a co-founder is caught up in fraudulent actions or seriously breaches the company's rules—like abusing her power, behaving badly with team members, or mishandling company funds—and as a result, she is shown the door. In situations like this, it is crucial she forfeits all her shares, no matter whether they have vested or not.

Following her exit, the company must swiftly take steps to repair any harm her actions may have caused. Communicating quickly and clearly with the rest of the team is key to rebuilding trust. Moreover, if her wrongdoing crosses into legal territory, like significant fraud or gross mismanagement, the company should consider taking legal action. Doing so not only cleans up the company's reputation but also reaffirms a commitment to integrity among the remaining team members.

Founders' Agreement

Forced Leave due to non-performance

When a co-founder is shown the door because she did not meet performance expectations, the big question is what happens to her shares. Does she get to keep all the shares she has earned up to that point, lose everything, or keep just a portion of those vested shares?

Before answering this, let us go back to the educational startup case study. Since we will be referring to this case in detail now, let us give names to the co-founders for clarity of communication. Let us say Jack and Ajay were the Engineers and Raj was the designer and CEO. Together they formed the engineering or the product team. The fourth co-founder who decided to join in late, let us name her Zane. In the original example, Zane had agreed to work part-time. The idea was that, with Zane's help, the engineering team would refine the product in the next three months post which Zane would go all out to sell the product to schools in her network while the product team would continue to provide support to customers. Let us say, additionally, Zane had committed that she should be able to get at least 20 schools on board in less than one year and another 100 in year two. Against this promise, the three co-founders had mutually agreed to share

10% of their startups' Equity with Zane split equally over a vesting period of two years.

Initially, the going was good. Zane was able to setup demo sessions with multiple schools. The feedback received through these sessions proved extremely useful in refining the product. Finally, after six months of hustling, the engineering team delivered a working product to Zane that she could go and sell to the schools in her network.

Once Zane had the product, she went all out and signed up the first two schools in the next month. However, the software implementation did not turn out as smoothly as everyone had expected. There were multiple bugs, and most of Zane's time was getting wasted in coordinating between the school and the product team.

By the end of nine months, only five schools were on board. There was a pipeline, but it did not seem promising. The discussions amongst the co-founders were getting heated by the day with no success in sight. Zane continued to blame a poor product and shady implementation, leading to the absence of any good references or client feedback for the low acceptance rate. Jack and Ajay felt that all the teething troubles had been resolved, and Zane was not doing enough to sell the product. Raj

Founders' Agreement

believed that the fault lied with all three of them and tried unsuccessfully to get the three of them to work together as a team.

It was evident that the team had failed to function together, and Zane had failed miserably in delivering on her promise. Only three months were due before her first-year shares would vest, so Zane decided to drag for a little more time. The split widened even further, and after bearing for another couple of months, Raj asked Zane to leave on the grounds of non-performance about a month before her shares would vest.

What is a fair outcome for Zane's equity under these circumstances? On one hand, she didn't hit the sales targets she promised, which could argue for her not receiving any shares. On the other, the other co-founders also fell short by not delivering a fully polished product as promised, which could support her case for keeping her due share. Then, there is the timing of her dismissal—just shy of her shares vesting. This move could be seen as opportunistic, suggesting she might deserve some portion of her equity for the work she did put in, like her role in product development and securing a few initial school contracts.

Conversely, consider the months Zane may

have spent biding time, while Raj independently hustled to secure sales from five additional schools—a task that, arguably, fell within Zane's remit. While Ajay, Jack, and Zane were caught up in a blame game, Raj took proactive steps to salvage the situation, succeeding where Zane had not. With Raj stepping up to cover for Zane's lack of action, does that not diminish her claim to the equity about to vest?

Try answering these questions after the events have already transpired, and you will never be able to arrive at an answer that will be agreeable to both Zane and the three other co-founders.

The crux of the matter hinges on whether Zane should receive none, all, or some percentage of her shares that were on the verge of vesting. If your answer is partial share for Zane, no matter how hard one tries, the split is bound to create hard feelings, will burn bridges and leave painful memories for both parties feeling short-changed. These kinds of disputes often stem from not having clear guidelines in place. This is particularly true for getting part-time co-founders, who are treading in two boats, are not willing to share equal risk, and whom you are roping in against a promise of certain specific deliverables they have sold you on. These scenarios should ideally get covered in the founder's agreement.

Let us say there was a provision that covered this scenario in the founder's agreement. Using those provisions, let us say, Zane is allowed to keep 50% of her vested shares, equating to 2.5% of the company, thus forfeiting the remaining 7.5% of her anticipated ownership. This leads us to another unresolved issue: what happens to the 7.5% of the company shares Zane leaves behind?

These shares would typically be redistributed back into the founders' pool. Let us understand the concept in detail.

Founders Pool

The founder's pool is the portion of shares in a company that is shared amongst the co-founders. Typically, at the outset of a startup, the founders hold 100% of the company's shares. However, as the company seeks funding, they may sell a portion of their shares to investors across several funding rounds. Additionally, founders might set aside a portion of their shares to create a pool they can later distribute amongst deserving employees to make them part owners and ensure that the employees remain motivated and get financial rewards linked to the company's growth.

As such, the ownership of the equity in a startup can be viewed as divided into three distinct groups: the founders, the employees, and the investors. This structure helps balance the interests and incentives of all parties involved in the company's growth.

Having understood the concept of founders' pool, let us now go back to the problem at hand. Specifically, who stands to inherit the 7.5% of the company's shares that are freed up once Zane exits the scene?

Founders' Agreement

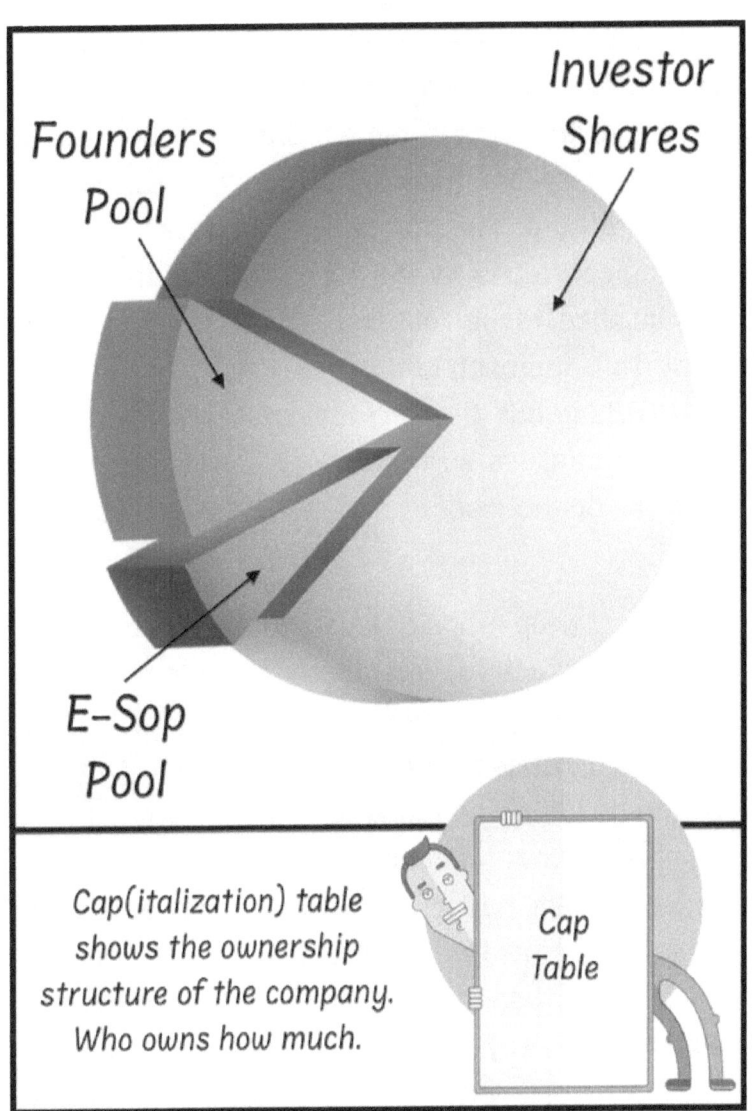

Cap(italization) table shows the ownership structure of the company. Who owns how much.

Founders' Agreement

To tackle this, let us revisit our ongoing discussion. The core question should be: What was the startup aiming to gain from the 10% equity originally allocated to Zane? Following Zane's departure, numerous responsibilities she was supposed to manage remain unaddressed. Going forward, someone has to pick up where Zane left off to ensure the company continues to thrive. The logical step is for the 7.5% of shares that Zane relinquished to be reabsorbed into the founders' pool. This approach not only makes up for the gap left by Zane but also provides a reserve of equity that can be allocated to future team members who will take on the responsibilities Zane was unable to fulfill.

The startup should leverage this reserve of equity to attract new members to the team, either as late-stage co-founders or to bring in outstanding management talent to compensate for the gap left by the departing co-founder. If there's any portion of this equity that remains unallocated till a liquidity event happens (like a company sale, IPO, future investments etc.), it could be re-distributed among the existing co-founders on a proportional basis. That way the equity goes back to the founders from whose pool the share was initially carved out.

Founders' Agreement

Scenario 2 – Mid-term Join

How to deal with ownership issues when a founder joins mid-term? There will be many such cases, especially in bootstrapped companies. Initially small, these ventures may reach a point where expanding the founding team becomes strategic for further growth. Determining the share of ownership to offer this new entrant hinges on several factors: the current growth phase of the business, the unique value the incoming co-founder contributes, and the sacrifices or opportunity costs they incur by joining. To grasp this better, let us go through a couple of examples that can give a directionalview to handling such scenarios.

Example 1

The startup is a couple of years old, with a solid business model, developed product lines, initial market traction, and it is ready to scale significantly. At this stage, the early stage risks typical of startups have largely been mitigated. So, what would be a fair shareof equity for a new co-founder coming on board now, someone who is facing considerably less career risk by joining?

This should be an easier one if the company already has a valuation. The guiding principle should be to structure the compensation so that the opportunity cost of the incumbent is taken care of, and then there is a decent upside that the incumbent should be able to make owing to her contribution to the Startup.

For example, let us say the company's equity comprises 10,000 shares. Each share is currently valued at ₹1,000 per share. As per the business plan, it is supposed to rise to ₹10,000 per share in the next three years. The opportunity cost for the incoming candidate is ₹300,000. One way to structure the compensation in this scenario will be to offer ₹200,000 in salary and another ₹200,000 worth in equity. So, the candidate ends up with 200 shares of the Startup. Over the next three years, the candidate should make ₹600,000 in salary and another ₹18,00,000 by way of share appreciation. Overall, the candidate will earn ₹24,00,000 over the next three years against the current opportunity cost of ₹900,000. (To simplify calculations, no annual increment has been considered in both cases.)

Example 2

If a startup is quite new, say under six months old, or if it's been around for a bit but has not nailed down its business model or developed a stable product, thena new co-founder stepping in is essentially taking on a substantial risk. Sometimes, the whole point of bringing someone new onboard is exactly for their potential to spur growth or wrap up product development.

In such a scenario, the incoming incumbent should betreated at almost par with the existing co-founders withsome time-based valuation discount. One must include the time-based value discount to honor the contribution of those who took the courage to risk everything and created a platform for the incumbent co-founder to join and perform.

For example, let us say the company's equity comprises 10,000 shares. Each share is currently valued at ₹100 per share. As per the business plan, it is supposed to rise to ₹10,000 per share in the next five years. The opportunity cost for the incoming candidate is ₹300,000. Given the early-stage nature of the Startup, the co-founders have capped their salary at ₹100,000 each. The founder is willing to share 30% equity with theincumbent co-founder. So, the candidate ends up with 3,000 shares of the Startup. Over the next three years, the candidate should make ₹300,000 in salary and another

₹2,97,00,000 by way of share appreciation. Overall,

Founders' Agreement

the candidate will earn ₹ 3,00,00,000 over the next three years against the current opportunity cost of ₹ 9,00,000.

Notice the stark difference in potential earnings between joining early versus later? In the first scenario, joining a more established startup yields ₹24,00,000, a 167% increase over the opportunity cost. In the second, joining at an earlier, riskier stage could lead to a 3,233% gain, making roughly ₹3,00,00,000.

Overall, if she joins the StartUp early, she is likely to make 12.5 times more money than if she joins the StartUp at a later date.

In the journey of co-founders in a startup, so far, we have covered the beginning and matters related to deciding on a fair split of equity when different individuals come together to form a Startup. Once the Startup is active, there will be instances when the views of co-founders will differ on various aspects. As a result, conflicts will arise, and if they are not settled, it may lead to underperformance of the Startup and even risk breaking up the founding team. In the next section of this book, we'll delve into strategies for resolving co- founder conflicts, ensuring the startup journey does not get derailed by internal disputes.

Founders' Agreement

Remember grandma's advice. The early bird gets the worm.
Start early to gain more.

Founders' Agreement

Conflict resolution

What about the scenario wherein co-founders disagree on something? There will be plenty of moments in your journey wherein things will not go as planned. Situations in which you will need to decide about course correction, changes in business model, pivoting, asking some early employees to leave, and like. Chances are that the co-founders will have different views on the best course of action on matters like these. And this will happen more than once. In fact, the more it happens, the better it will be for the company in the long run. That is because if the idea is thrashed out amongst the team in-depth, chances of surprises and disagreements going forward will be minimal. The question we need to answer is how to deal with such situations, especially when you have an early investor on board.

An essential task for any early stage founding team is fostering an environment where questioning and open dialogue are encouraged. This challenge might seem daunting, particularly for individuals raised in hierarchical cultures or educated in traditional settings, like many schools in India, where questioning authority isn't the norm. It may indeed be difficult to undo years of training of subversion and following the authority, but that is a must for any startup to succeed, and the responsibility to encourage or create such a culture

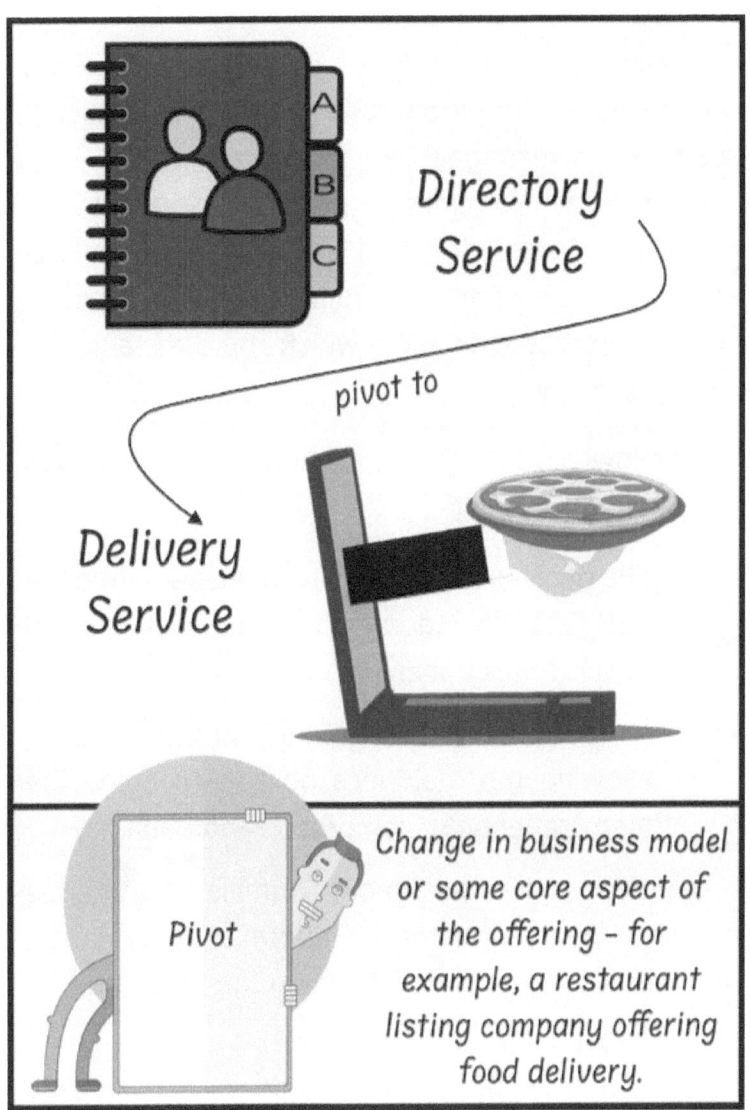

lies entirely on the shoulders of the co-founders and early stage employees.

With such a culture in place, reaching consensus on important issues through discussion becomes manageable. However, there will inevitably be moments when the way forward isn't clear-cut. Sometimes, you are faced with several options, each appearing as viable as the next. In these instances, deciding which route to take can be perplexing.

Following are a few possible ways to solve such a conundrum.

1. The decision falls to the team leader, often the CEO, with the understanding that everyone will support the chosen direction.

2. A decision could be made through a vote, allowing the majority's opinion to guide the team, reflecting a democratic approach.

3. The individual most familiar with the problem—whether due to proximity, expertise, or responsibility for enacting the solution—has the final say.

4. The person charged with achieving the outcome in question is granted the decision-making power.

Founders' Agreement

You may choose to adopt any of these strategies or perhaps some entirely benign strategy. Different scenarios might call for different approaches, and there's no universally correct answer that would apply to every scenario. Personally, I lean towards option four, with option three as a close second. Initially, I often resorted to voting, but as time went on, I moved away from either using or recommending that method, especially in the early stages of the startup.

As to why I moved away from using the democratic set-up, through experience, in the early days of a startup, I would say that running a startup is akin to navigating through a battlefield. You're working with limited resources, leading a small team, facing competition on multiple fronts, and making decisions with minimal information. This environment is hardly the place for a full-blown democracy.

Imagine if your soldiers (team) collectively decide not to fight on weekends, irrespective of what is happening to their territory (company) during that time. Such a laid-back approach is unsustainable in an early-stage startup, particularly a bootstrapped one with limited resources.

Founders' Agreement

Founders' Agreement

What about the first approach, in which the CEO decides, and everyone follows? There could be situations wherein a leader commits to a path that other co-founders have not bought into. This situation may lead to dissatisfaction amongst the team. The dissenting members may not remain committed to the action plan. In the worst-case scenario, they may stop cooperating altogether. There is a possibility that a few of them may even secretly wish for the plan to fail, to prove that they had been right all the way. This situation can arise in any team, not just amongst co-founders. Such a dynamic, if it is allowed to exist, will be disastrous for the team.

In situations of disagreement, it is crucial for every team member to remember why the team leader was chosen in the first place. By joining the team, they bought into the leader's vision. If the leader is reasonable, if the conflicting options have been discussed and thrashed out at length, and if there is no clear winner amongst the conflicting options even after that, it is best to go with the leader's decision. Ultimately, the leader carries the burden of the startup's success on their shoulders. Once a decision is reached, everyone should commit fully to its execution irrespective of their initial position. This is where embracing the

Founders' Agreement

Founders' Agreement

principle of "Agree to Disagree" becomes valuable.

Within our context, "Agree to Disagree" means that while team members may have their reservations about a particular course of action, once a decision is finalized, they accept it as a unified choice and begin to regard it as their own. Co-founders and team members are free to discuss, argue, and express dissent behind closed doors. However, once a path is selected—be it through approach 1, 2, 3, or 4—that decision becomes the collective stance of the team. Moving forward, it is imperative that they present a united front when interacting with employees, other teams, and investors, ensuring consistent communication across all fronts.

If the larger team senses any conflict in decision making, it will pave the way for corporate politics to kick in, creating an opposing force that will be immensely difficult to deal with. Likewise, if investors catch wind that the team is not unified, it will present a whole new set of challenges to tackle.

So far, we have explored four methods for addressing conflicts. But what about a fifth option: consulting with investors for their input? Depending on the circumstances or the decision at hand, this could either be a risky move or a strategic one that might benefit the company significantly.

Founders' Agreement

When is it a terrible idea? If the issue at hand is relatively minor that does not warrant investor's time or focus, involving them could be an overstep. Secondly, if the matter is deeply technical and specific to your business—a field outside the investor's primary area of expertise—it might not be wise to solicit their advice.

Why could reaching out under these circumstances be ill-advised? Consider this: investors have put their faith and funds into your venture, relying on your team's deep understanding of the industry. They are savvy about finance and investment strategies, but you are the master of your domain, that is why they have invested in you. Asking them to weigh in on a niche technical issue might seed doubts about your team's capabilities. Further, presenting a disjointed front may additionally get them worried about if the team will stick together in the long run.

Way too many startups fail when unqualified people without any skin in-game, with little ground experience but fancy college degrees, whose only motive is to get fat paychecks and E-Sops, join startups post investor action, once the investors start losing faith in the founding team's ability to scale up. This situation can emerge if investors begin to question the original team's capacity to evolve and grow the business effectively.

Founders' Agreement

When is it a good idea? Seeking investors' opinions can be highly beneficial under the right circumstances. It's particularly useful when the input you need is strategic in nature, or when you're looking for broad, high-level advice on topics such as scaling your business, exploring new marketing strategies, entering new markets, or optimizing your distribution channels.

Why can turning to your investors for advice on these matters be a smart move? Simply put, investors typically have a wealth of experience with a variety of companies across different stages of growth and development. They are well-versed in the rhythms of business cycles and understand what it takes to successfully scale a venture. Their extensive networks can be invaluable, offering shortcuts in your learning journey, facilitating introductions to potential clients, or setting up crucial meetings. Moreover, their insights are often grounded in the patterns and outcomes they have observed across their investment portfolio, providing you with perspectives and advice that are both relevant and tested.

Whenever you approach investors, remember two mantras.

1. Whenever you reach out to investors for their opinion on conflicting approaches, present a

collective front. Discuss as a team, don't discuss the approaches at an individual level giving any impression of disagreement amongst the team.

2. Don't ask open-ended questions without sharing the information that may help them decide. For example, if you are presenting two conflicting approaches, also mention the pros and cons of both and then seek their advice for your team to be able to decide on the best approach.

In such a scenario, the investor may share their views or help you connect with some expert in the field who can help you decide or give you a general direction to think through or may ask you to do some specific analysis or gather some specific data points that may help you reach the right decision. This will be far better than the alternative scenario wherein you discuss the two options at an individual level, cut other team members and give the investor an impression of a dysfunctional unit that cannot work together, much less scale up and take the startup to success.

However, if, despite your best intentions, an impasse is reached that results in a co-founder's departure, it is important to manage the situation gracefully, ensuring the exit is amicable. Additionally, you will need to put several safeguards in place to ensure that there is minimal damage to the team and the company going forward.

In the next section, we will delve into the considerations and actions necessary when a co-founder decides to leave.

Founders' Agreement

When a Founder Quits

In the unfortunate event of a co-founder leaving the team, apart from losing a critical resource, the company may also have to deal with a high order of business risk. This is because the exiting co-founder will have a considerable amount of information with her that she can use to the company's detriment. For example, she would be familiar with your vendors and suppliers, understand who your clients are, know the ins and outs of your operational processes, be aware of any weaknesses, and she will also be privy to the company's future plans.

Typically, nobody joins a startups' founding team with the intent of leaving early. If a co-founder is exiting prematurely, it is likely the separation is not amicable. Such situations can lead to feelings of resentment, a sense of injustice, and anger. Given that state of mind, what is going to prevent her from aligning with a competitor, starting a rival business, or at the very least, spreading negative information about the startup? This could deter potential customers and damage the business's future. This scenario is quite common, especially in small or early-stage startups that have begun to scale and secure funding.

To safeguard against these risks, it is crucial to anticipate and address potential exit scenarios within the founders' agreement. Ensuring that matters such as confidentiality, intellectual property rights, defamation, and competition are clearly outlined; can help prevent such fallout. The next sections will delve into these critical areas, offering guidance on how to protect the startup and maintain a fair and respectful environment, even in the wake of a co-founder's departure.

Confidential Information

Confidential information is often defined in elaborate legal terms, sometimes too complex and confusing for anyone to understand what it means. In layman's terms, any information which is not in the public domain (read publicly available to people outside your company) and which you are privy to because of your role in the company; comprises confidential information. This applies irrespective of the fact whether the information is essential or trivial or whether you feel it should be protected or not.

It is crucial to have a confidentiality agreement in place, not just among co-founders but also with early stage employees and anyone else who might handle sensitive data. This ensures that everyone

Founders' Agreement

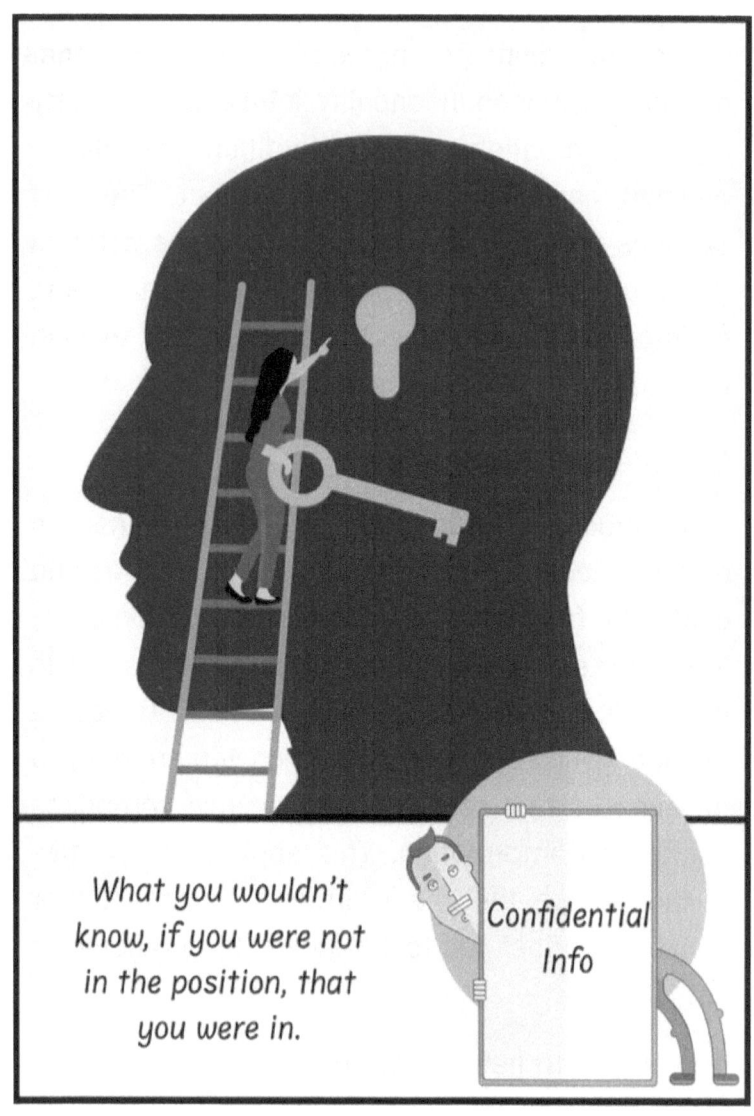

understands the importance of keeping this information under wraps and the legal implications of disclosing it.

Intellectual Property

Intellectual Property, or IP, offers startups a significant edge in the competitive landscape. IP can manifest in various forms, such as patents, copyrights, trademarks, and design rights, among others. Delving into the specifics of each type is not something we will do in this book. For a basic and raw understanding, consider anything created afresh, which did not exist before, is not predominantly a copy of something else, to be intellectual property. This includes elements like logos, websites, gadgets, designs, inventions, and so forth, all falling under the broad umbrella of IP. There are more detailed categories based on the type of IP—like patents for inventions, copyrights for literary and artistic works, trademarks for brand identity, etc.—which we won't go into here. For those keen on digging deeper into how to build an Intellectual Property Portfolio, the book "1-hour Startup-tool kit – Creating an Intellectual Property (IP) Portfolio" offers a wealth of information on the topic.

Founders' Agreement

Original work, registered and protected by law.

Intellectual Property

Founders' Agreement

Let us now try to understand What role does Intellectual Property (IP) play, and why is it so crucial fora company?

Essentially, owning an IP, grants to the owner, exclusive legal rights to use and control the IP. Consider this scenario: your startup has gained momentum, attracting a significant customer base that recognizes you, buys from you regularly, and even promotes you through word-of-mouth. To ensure your customers can distinctly identify your brand, you have invested in creating an eye-catching pictorial logo that has begun to symbolize your company in the minds of consumers. Then, one fine day, you are served a notice stating you can no longer use your logo because it is too similarto that of a lesser-known entity located in a remote corner of your country. Despite having designed the logo yourself, it never crossed your mind to officially register it and secure your ownership rights.

IP rights function as assets, similar to other types of assets, and are inherently linked to ownership. If the startup itself holds the IP rights to an asset, it has the exclusive authority not only to utilize that asset but also to legally prevent any copycats or counterfeiters from using it.

However, consider the scenario where the IP asset

Founders' Agreement

Dukaan and khatabook, two funded startups, were involved in a long legal tussle over trademark violation which was eventually settled out of court.

 Before choosing a logo, tag line or brand name – do check is someone else has already trademarked it.

Founders' Agreement

WeWork ended up paying millions of dollars to its own CEO to use the word 'We'

Ensure that the intellectual property is owned by the startup and not by individual employees.

is owned by individual founders or co-founders rather than the startup as a whole. What if the owner of the IP asset is a founder who decides to leave the company, and the departure is under less than amicable circumstances. Think of the trouble that this can ensue in the long run.

Defamation

Your co-founder has in-depth knowledge of critical aspects of your business, including key customers, vendors, and the pipeline of potential customers. She might even be the primary contact for some of these relationships. Thus, if a co-founder turns against the startup and begins to speak negatively about it, the repercussions could be severe, both materially and financially.

Negative commentary from a central figure within the startup is likely to be taken very seriously by its network. Imagine, for instance, rumors spread that the co-founder has left due to fraud, financial mismanagement, or because the startup is supposedly running out of funds and is on the brink of collapse within three months. If such claims are attributed to a member of the founding team, the best-case scenario might involve the loss of potential future clients. However, the consequences could extend far more significantly, potentially

Founders' Agreement

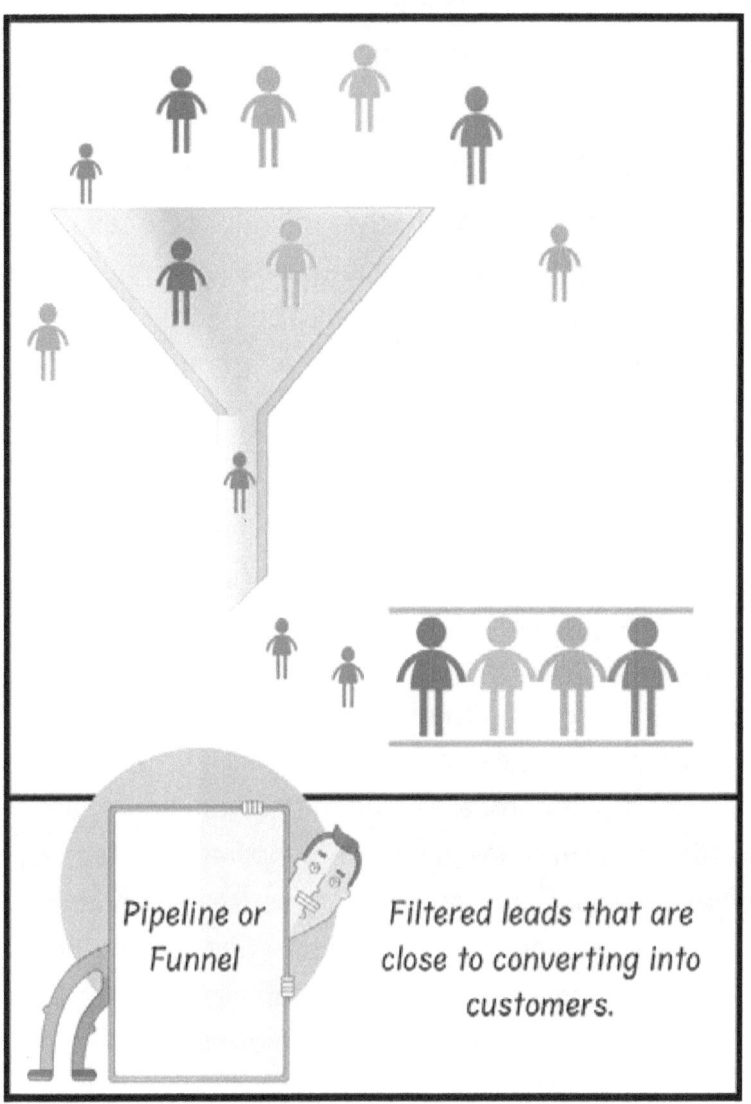

resulting in the loss of current clients and vendor relationships. Additionally, any setback for the startup could inadvertently benefit its competitors.

Non-Compete

Navigating through these kinds of scenarios might seem daunting, but they are manageable. Trust me. Yes, there will be hard feelings, moments of resentment, bitterness, and frustration. Tempers will run high. However, over time, the individual will find peace and calm will prevail.

But let us consider a more challenging situation: what if the departing individual dedicates herself to becoming a direct competitor, fueled by a desire to challenge the startup she perceives as having wronged her? What if she channels all her energies, finances, and waking hours to building a startup that competes with her previous company? Armed with knowledge of suppliers, customers, operational processes, employees, marketing strategies, and sensitive information, she is well-prepared to compete. Her established reputation and connections from her time at the startup give her a significant head start. She can avoid past mistakes without the cost of learning them firsthand, thanks to her insider perspective. This

Founders' Agreement

scenario can evolve into a formidable challenge, presenting a real nightmare for the original startup.

Even in scenarios where a co-founder exits on good terms, the possibility of them launching a rival startup poses a significant threat. Such a venture could swiftly evolve into a strong competitor. You would not want that to happen ever to your Startup. And this holds not only for co-founders but also for early-stage employees and all the key management personnel in your Startup. Therefore, incorporating a non-compete clause in the founders' agreement is essential.

A non-compete clause, in principle, means that any departing co-founder or key employee agrees not to enter into or start a similar business that competes with the startup, typically for a specified period ranging from two to four years. This restriction encompasses not only the establishment of a competing business but also prohibits joining another company that operates in the same domain or offers exactly similar or substitute products.

Founders' Agreement

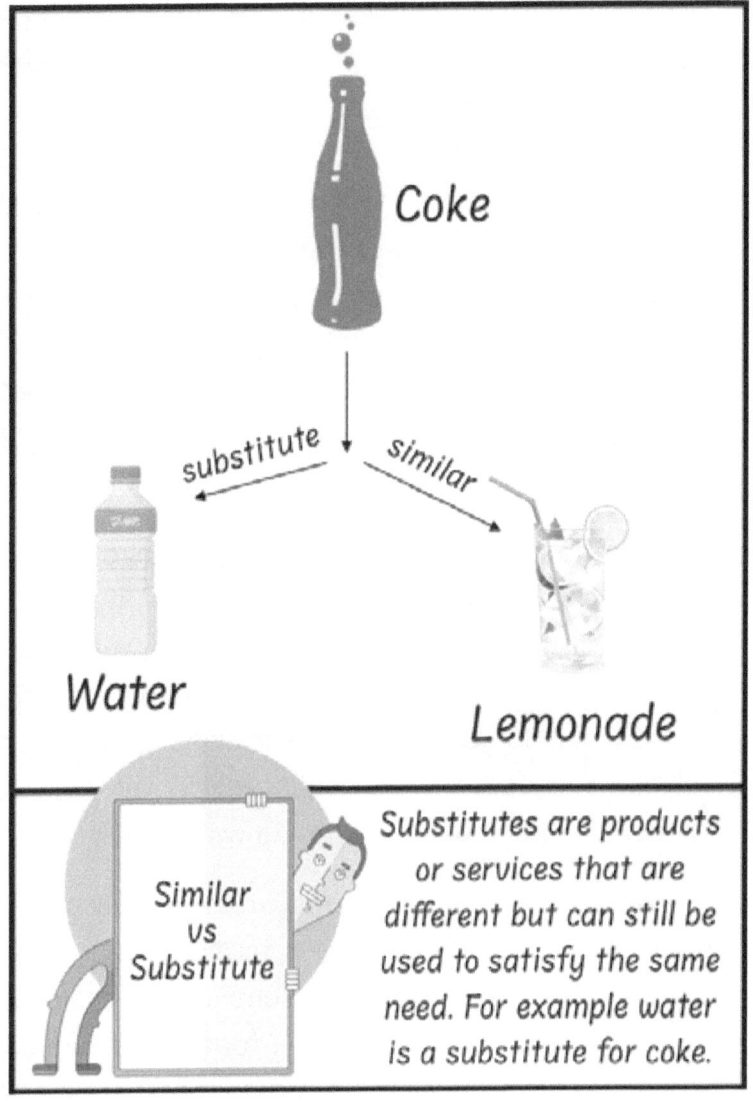

Restriction on sale or transfer

So, you have added enough safeguards in the founders' agreement to ensure that no harm comes to the company once a co-founder leaves. The departing co-founder is fully aware of these precautions, which is why she contemplates selling all her shares before her exit. She knows she will get an attractive price if she sells the shares to a competitor. If not to a competitor, she can at least sell these to any other investor. After all, she has lost faith in the business model and does not believe that the Startup is headed in the right direction.

The question of whether she should be permitted to sell her shares is crucial. One would feel that the Startup and the leaving co-founder would have very different opinion on how to handle this issue, but you would be surprised to find, that in all likelihood, their approaches will be aligned, depending upon whether the exit was good or bad.

An exit is considered good when the leaving co-founder departs on amicable terms. The reason for her departure may be personal or professional, or situational, but she has performed her duties, trained other employees, remained transparent and has dealt with the matter of her leaving in a professional manner.

An exit is considered bad when the co-founder leaves because she has lost faith in business, or is told to leave due to performance issues, under contentious circumstances, or on other hostile grounds.

Good Exit

In case of a good exit, in all probability, the co-founder who is exiting the Startup feels a strong sense of pride in what she has contributed, remains emotionally connected to the company, and retains faith in its future success. Under these circumstances, she might prefer to keep her shares, looking forward to benefiting from the startup's future growth.

From the startup's perspective, maintaining a relationship with this co-founder could be highly beneficial. They might see value in her continued involvement, perhaps in a mentorship or advisory role, leveraging her goodwill and expertise to further support the startup's journey. Given the safeguards already in place within the founders' agreement to mitigate potential downsides, the startup would not typically be concerned about having a former co-founder as a shareholder. In essence, she would become another early-stage investor, offering her support and investment in the company's continued success.

Bad Exit

In the event of an unfavorable exit, the situation can unfold in two ways: either the co-founder decides to leave due to a loss of confidence in the startup's direction, or she is compelled to exit following a strained separation. In either case, her outlook on the company's future prospects might be dim. So, in all likelihood, she would want to sell out the shares and get whatever gains she can get before it is too late as per her diagnosis.

From the startup's standpoint, it is obligated to disclose certain information and updates to all shareholders. However, if the departure was acrimonious, the startup might not be keen on the idea of the exiting co-founder retaining her shares and be privy to this information. Consequently, the company might be more inclined to facilitate her desire to sell or otherwise relinquish her shares, allowing both parties to sever ties more cleanly.

If you look at it closely, you will notice that irrespective of whether the exit is good or bad, the desired outcome that both the Startup and the co-founder want to achieve is the same. In the event of a favorable exit, accompanied by ongoing faith in the startup's potential, both parties may prefer to maintain their connection. This continuity not only benefits them but also projects a reassuring message to the wider community, that even those who are leaving the company, still believes in its potential.

Conversely, following a less amicable departure, neither the startup nor the co-founder is typically interested in continuing their association. The co-founder would wish to encash at the earliest. At the same time, the Startup would not want to deal with the departing co-founder in future and would like to eliminate even the remotest possibility of her creating any trouble in the long run.

That is why it is imperative to cover the matter of exchange of shares (whether by sale, or gift, or transfer) in the founder's agreement. Ideally, a founder should not be allowed to sell or transfer the shares to anyone but to the company, other co-founders, or existing investors. However, this approach might not always be equitable to the departing co-founder, who could potentially secure a higher offer from an external party. Maybe someone outside is willing to offer her a much larger amount as compared to what her Startup and co-founders are offering. And this outsider is not even a competitor, but a reputed investor who could be a good strategic addition to the startup, who may help build the company in the long run. Shouldn't she get a fair price, then?

Here, I am sharing two possible approaches to deal with this issue.

Approach 1

Tying the share price to the most recent round of valuation. This approach seems straightforward and efficient at first glance; however, this method can present challenges depending on the timing of the last valuation and the subsequent performance of the business.

For the departing founder, this strategy might not reflect well if the last valuation wasn't recent, and the business has since experienced significant growth. She will end up selling her shares at a significant discount to their fair market price.

Conversely, the startup might find itself at a disadvantage if the most recent valuation was particularly high and the company has failed to meet the growth expectations set during that round.

In this case, the startup will end up paying a much higher price for buying back its shares irrespective of the business reality.

This mismatch can lead to complications for either party, underscoring the need for a more dynamic approach to determining share prices that accurately reflects the current state and potential of the business.

Approach 2

The second approach which is more balanced, gives to the startup, a Right of First Refusal (RoFR) to any competing offer brought in by the departing co-founder.

Here is how it works. The departing co-founder is permitted to seek buyers outside the company (with the exception of competitors or entities specifically prohibited by the startup's agreements). Once she secures a bona fide offer from an external buyer, she must present this offer to the board, allowing them the opportunity to match the buyer's price. If the board, co- founders, or current investors can meet this offer, the exiting co-founder is obligated to sell her shares to them instead.

Founders' Agreement

Founders' Agreement

On the other hand, if they cannot match the offer, she is free to proceed with the sale to the external buyer, who then becomes a new shareholder or investor in the company.

With this, we have navigated through the three pivotal stages of founder interactions: when they come together and decide how to split the equity, when they work together and decide how to deal with conflicts, and when they quit and choose how to deal with balance equity. Now, it's time for us to say goodbye.

I hope that the time you have invested in reading this book has been worthwhile and that you had something new to learn. If it was, and if you think of someone whom this book can help, do recommend it to them.

It is always good to help someone.

Take care, and I wish you the very best in your startup endeavors.

Founders' Agreement Template

As promised, shared next is a template for a founders' agreement that you can use for your startup idea. In many cases, the co-founders first come together to work on an idea without forming any legal entity. The company is formed at a later date when the idea has shaped up or reached some milestone. If your situation is similar, you should incorporate that fact in your founders' agreement and ensure that the agreement clearly tackles the issue of transfer of IP from founders to the Company.

These kinds of scenarios, however, do leave room for future conflict and chances of renegotiation or reneging on the initial understanding. The added legal cost of a multi-step process is another issue that the company/founders will have to bear in such a case. I would suggest forming a legal entity or, at the minimum, documenting the intent to do so in the founders' agreement.

The agreement draft we will be covering assumes the existence of the legal entity at the time of signing the founders' agreement.

Founders' Agreement

Disclaimer

Please note that I have referred to different resources available in the public domain and edited them to create a simple and holistic template. I have tried to refrain from using complex legal language and avoided legal jargon wherever possible. I have kept the template simple on purpose, to ensure that it is easy to understand and implement so that the startup founders do not have to burn their pockets by paying high attorney fees for drafting one. This is not a legal document or substitute for one.

Annexure A

This Founders' Agreement (the "Agreement") effective from [DD/MM/YYYY] is entered into by [Company Name] (the "Company"), and [Founder 1 Name], [Founder 2 Name], [Founder n Name] collectively referred to as the "Founders."

Now, the Company and the Founders agree as follows:

Business Idea

The Founders have developed the business idea of *[give a brief of the core business idea]*. They have created [Company Name] to implement the business idea. The Company's registration number is [Company's registration No.].

Capital Contribution

The following table lists the capital contribution being brought in by each of the Fou

Founder	Contribution	Currency
Founder 1		
Founder 2		
.		
Founder N		
Total		

The capital contribution is meant to support Company's expenses and is not refundable.

Additional capital contributions may be made in the future subject to the mutual consent of the Founders.

Ownership Structure

The ownership of the Company will be divided amongst the Founders as follows:

Founder	Ownership %age
Founder 1	
Founder 2	
.	
Founder N	
Total	

[The total ownership held by the Founders will constitute the "Founders Pool."]

Ownership Vesting

The ownership issued to each Founder shall vest over a period of [Number] Years starting [DD/MM/YYYY] on a/an [Monthly/Quarterly/Annual] basis at a proportionalrate.

If a Founder ceases to be the Founder for any reason, the unvested ownership of that Founder will be returned to the [Company/Founders Pool].

Founders' Salary

For the first year, starting [DD/MM/YYYY], the founders will draw a fixed monthly salary as per the details given below:

Founder	Salary	Currency
Founder 1		
Founder 2		
.		
Founder N		
Total		

The salary may be revised after the first year by mutual consent of all the Founders.

Voting Rights

Each Founder will have voting rights proportional to their ownership percentage in the Company.

In the event of a split decision, [Founder x/the CEO] shall cast the deciding vote.

Ownership of Intellectual Property

The ownership of any Intellectual Property related to the business idea, whether already created or created in the future, by the Founders or by any third party on assignment by the Founders, shall reside with the Company.

Any provisions of this section shall not apply to any Intellectual Property developed by any Founder that is unrelated to the Business idea and is developed by the Founder entirely on their own time without using any of the Company's resources, including equipment, time, facilities and supplies.

Confidentiality

The Founders will ensure that the Business Idea and any information related to the Company that is not available freely in the public domain shall remain confidential. Disclosure of such information to any party shall occur only on a need basis and only after the mutual consent of all Founders.

Non-Compete

The Founders agree that as long as they are

employed with the Company and for a period of [Number] years thereafter, they will not start, join, or assist any business, group or individual that may be competing with the Company or offering products or services that may be of similar nature as that provided by the Company.

Resignation

Any Founder may cease employment with the Company by giving written notice of [Number] monthsto the Company.

Removal

Any Founder may be removed by [Number percentageof votes/majority vote] as per the voting provisions contained in this agreement.

Amendments and Termination

This agreement may only be amended or terminated by an agreement in writing signed by all Founders.

Representation and Warranties

Each Founder represents and warrants that they are not a part of any other agreement that will restrict them from performing their obligations as outlined in this agreement.

Severability

If a court holds any provision of this agreement as invalid or unenforceable, or illegal, the remaining provisions shall remain in full force and effect.

Choice of Jurisdiction

Founders agree that the courts of [State, Country] shall have exclusive jurisdiction to settle any claim or dispute arising out of or in connection with this Agreement.

Entire Agreement

All understandings and agreements, whether written or verbal, previously existing between the Founders, if any, are merged into this Agreement.

In Witness Whereof the Founders and the Company have caused this Agreement to be duly executed.

[Company Name]

_____

[Company Representative Name]

Founders' Agreement

[Position/Designation]

Founder 1

_____

[Founder 1 Name]

Founder 2

_____

[Founder 2 Name]

Founder N

_____

[Founder N Name]

Founders' Agreement

NOTES

Founders' Agreement

NOTES

www.ingramcontent.com/pod-product-compliance
Lightning Source LLC
Chambersburg PA
CBHW031425210526
45464CB00005B/2060